To,

Let's keep laughing !

HOW TO BE A

BIG
STRONG
MAN

HOW TO BE A

BIG STRONG MAN

A MODERN GUIDE TO MASCULINITY
BY SAMUEL LEIGHTON-DORE

Smith
Street
Books

A BIG STRONG INTRO

I know what you're thinking. *Finally*, a book about men.

Growing up, I was never the right kind of boy. My hair was too long, my mannerisms were too flouncy, and I was far too into Julie Andrews musicals. For years I was bullied, beaten and berated on the school playground because I didn't fit into the neat mould of how a boy should look or act. I was different. I had bits spilling over the edges, making a weird, colourful mess.

Despite being sensitive and kind, I quickly learned that these qualities – ones my parents had long nurtured and celebrated – made me an outcast. Why? Simply because they weren't seen as the way a boy should be – they were seen as *girly*. And for a while, I believed it. I believed it when I was told that boys should be strong; that boys shouldn't cry; that boys should get up to mischief; that boys shouldn't ask for help – that boys should just toughen up a bit.

None of this is a surprise, really. We're hammered with traditional notions of masculinity from the day we're born. The moment we're dropped into a blue onesie, assigned a football team and called a 'big boy', we're essentially screwed. If men are to truly flourish, free of expectations and projections, we need to realise that these ideals are no longer serving us – that, in fact, they're holding us back.

What if we were to unlearn our definitions of masculinity and strength? What if when we thought of the word 'strong' we thought of someone who was unafraid to share their vulnerabilities, rather than someone who can deadlift twice their body weight? What if when we thought of the word 'manly' we thought of someone who was comfortable in their own skin, rather than someone who felt the need to condescend, ridicule and dominate? To quote a pretty famous highly sensitive man: 'You may say I'm a dreamer, but I'm not the only one.'

How To Be A Big Strong Man is an innately optimistic collection of observations, jokes and ideas. It's a useful companion for boys, men, and those who love them. It's a scribbly, incomplete blueprint for how society could evolve if only we lowered our weapons, pushed through our knee-jerk defensiveness and accepted that some things have to change.

Toxic masculinity might be best explained as two men locking each other in the same tiny cage and then freaking out at anyone who walks by and looks at them funny. When we hold onto any concept too tightly – particularly something so tied to our identity, like gender – we lose all flexibility. This stiffness leaves us unequipped to not only accept other people, but to accept and express ourselves.

Let's open the fucking cage.

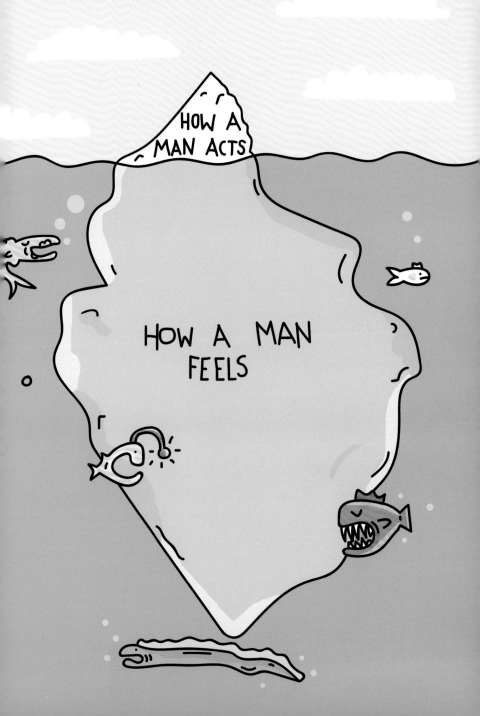

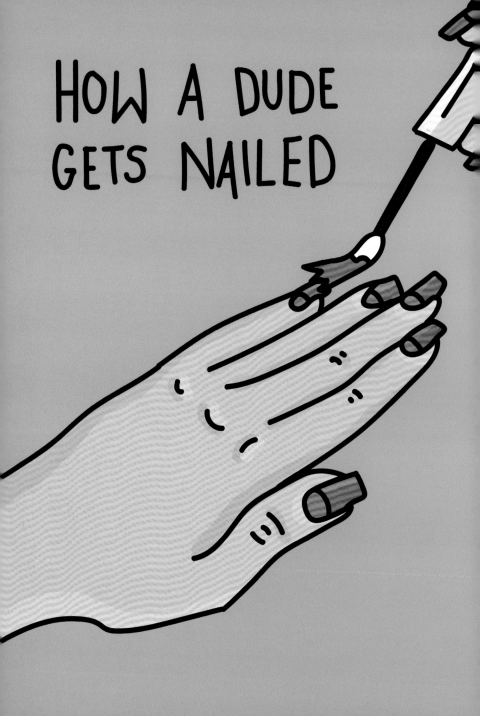

A TRIANGLE TRYING TO SQUEEZE
THROUGH A CIRCLE

WHERE MEN WITH
PANIC DISORDERS
SUPPORT ONE ANOTHER

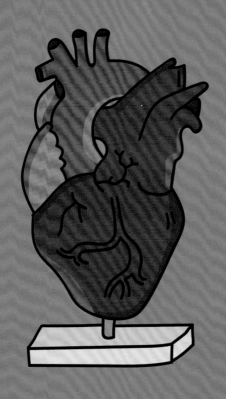

THE BIGGEST STRONGEST
MOST MANLY MUSCLE

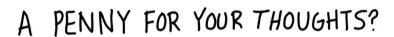

A PENNY FOR YOUR THOUGHTS?

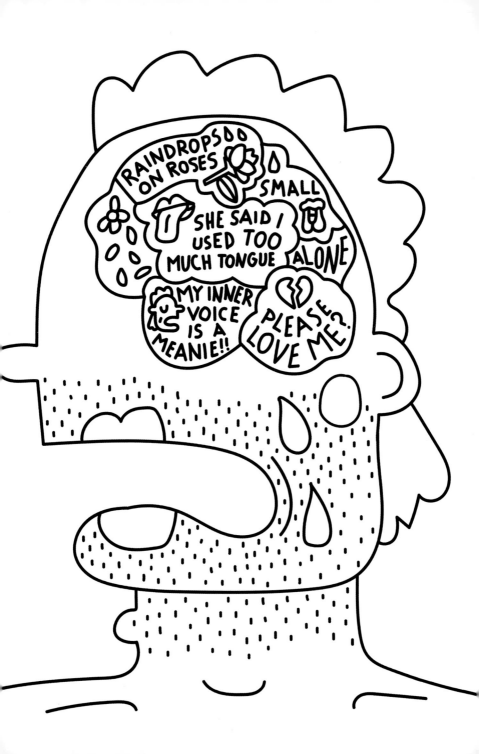

HOW TO THROW THE PERFECT GENDER REVEAL PARTY

A GYM FOR MEN

THE GUIDE TO MANHOOD

(THEY WEREN'T)

HOW TOXIC MASCULINITY BEGAN

UH-OH

SOME GREAT OPTIONS
FOR MAN-PARTS

THE NEWS

— INDEPENDENT— KIND OF —

WHY MEN HATE BEING LOOKED AT THE WRONG WAY...

ANGRY MAN GETS AWAY WITH IT (AGAIN) BY A MAN

THE LOUDER HE YELLS, THE BIGGER AND STRONGER HE FEELS — BUT THE SMALLER AND WEAKER HE LOOKS TO EVERYBODY ELSE. **CONTINUED, PAGE 7.**

SPORT STUFF

COACH CRIES AFTER LOSS, ENCOURAGES TEAMMATES TO HUG IT OUT ♥ ♥

INSIDE: MEN HUGGING!!!

MORE: PG 32

THE MOST MANLY EMOJIS

VERY MANLY WAYS TO GET AROUND

PHRENOLOGY OF THE DICK

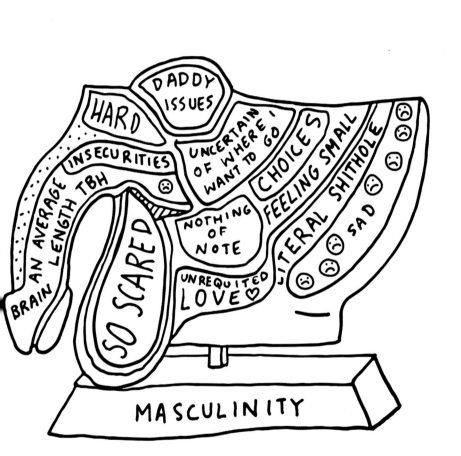

MAYBE PRISONERS GET TEARS TATTOOED ON THEIR FACES BECAUSE THEY'RE ACTUALLY BEING HELD CAPTIVE BY SOCIETY'S PROJECTION OF HOW THEY SHOULD EXPRESS THEMSELVES...

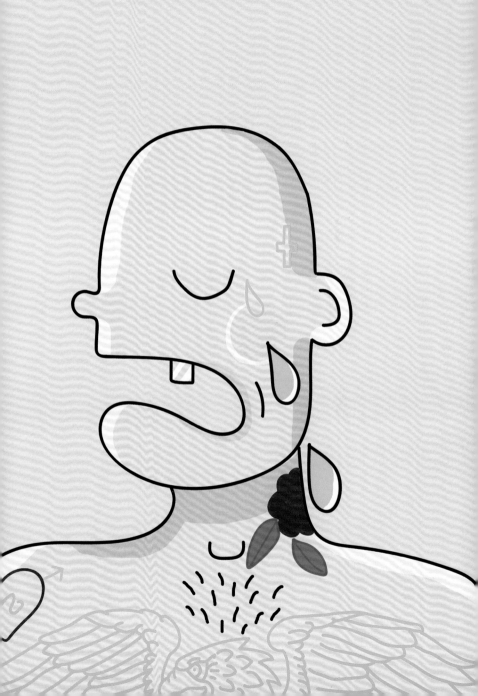

OUTSIDE

3 SUPER IMPORTANT
STEPS TO BEING
A SUPER IMPORTANT
MAN

1. IDENTIFY AS A MAN
2. DO IMPORTANT THINGS
   (LIKE HELP PEOPLE)
3. BE NICE, I GUESS?

A PUSH-UP

A HELP-UP

THINGS YOU WEREN'T TAUGHT
IN SEX ED

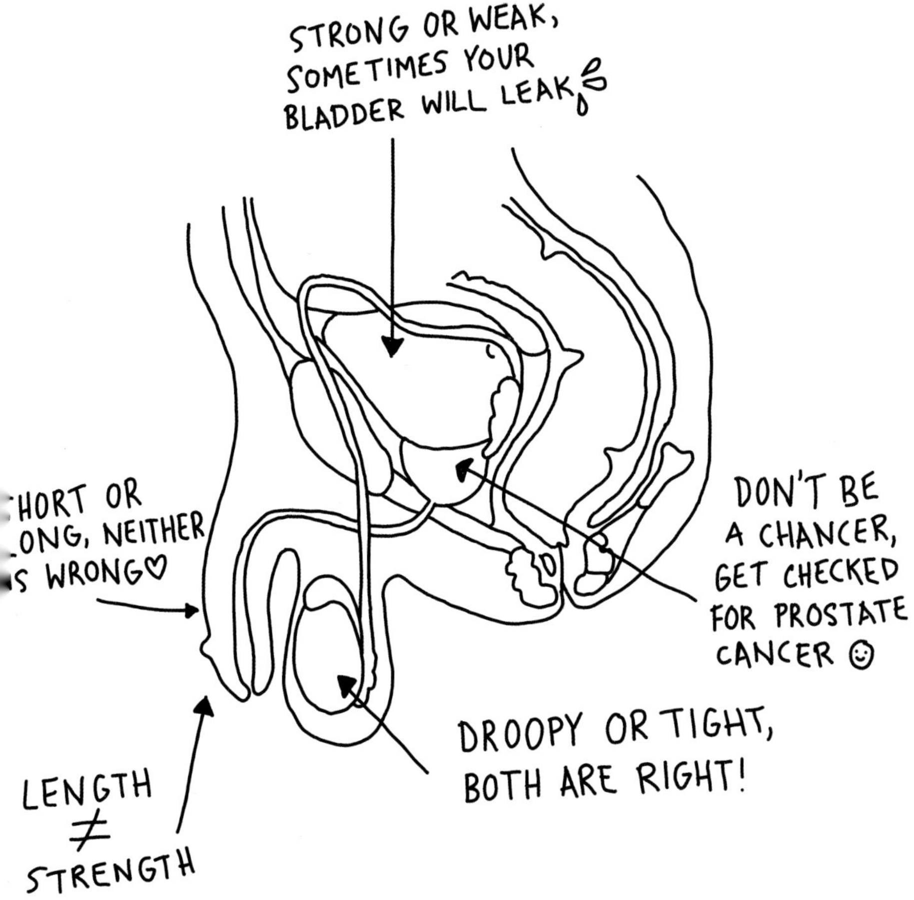

STRONG OR WEAK,
SOMETIMES YOUR
BLADDER WILL LEAK

HORT OR
ONG, NEITHER
S WRONG♡

DON'T BE
A CHANCER,
GET CHECKED
FOR PROSTATE
CANCER ☺

DROOPY OR TIGHT,
BOTH ARE RIGHT!

LENGTH
≠
STRENGTH

A SPORT STAR

ALSO A SPORT STAR

CLEO CENTREFOLD

A BIG STRONG MAN
USING THE IPHONE
'MEASURE' APP

(AND THEN CHOOSING
NOT TO SEND A DICK PIC)

Men's Health
MENTAL HEALTH ISSUE
WHY FEMINISM IS A TURN-ON
THE #1 MUSCLE
(HERE'S A CLUE: ♥)
25 WAYS TO ASK FOR HELP.
HOW TO FIND THE RIGHT PSYCH FOR YOU!
MUM
WORKOUTS
FOR YOUR MIND!!!
6 THINGS MORE IMPORTANT THAN THE CAR YOU DRIVE
BEING STRON
WHEN LIFE GETS HARD
MAKEUP FOR MEN!
REJECTION
HOW TO DEAL W/ IT...

THE MAGAZINE FOR BIG STRONG MEN
GQ
THRIVING WITH ANXIETY
mindfulness
TRANS GUYS TELL ALL
-LIFE
-LOVE
-SEX
ARE YOU LIVIN' LA VI DA Lonely?
10 ANGER REDUCTION TECHNIQUES
DEPRESSION AND SEX
RADICAL CONSENT
YES! YES!
help!
M LITTLE
OWN THERE...

WHAT MAKES A MAN ATTRACTIVE?

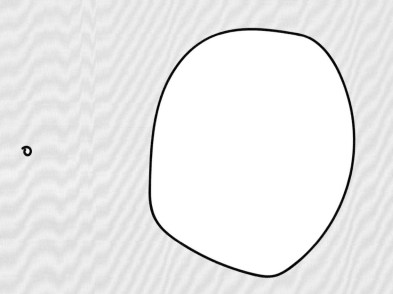

HOW LOUD HE CAN
SHOUT FROM A MOVING
VEHICLE

—HOW KIND HE
IS

HIS ABILITY TO DO
THAT DANCING PECS
WIBBLE-WOBBLE CHEST
THING

HOW HEAVY HE SQUATS

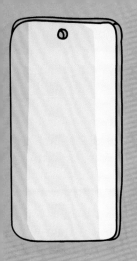

VERY PERSONAL TRAINING

HOW TO WRESTLE WITH HARD FEELINGS

MEN

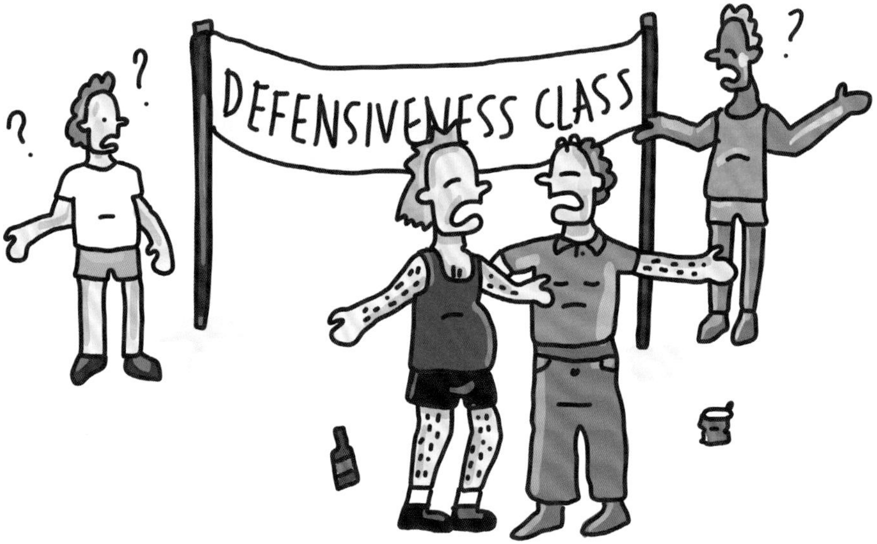

WOMEN

And then the prince affirmed his gender and rescued himself...

" THERE'S NOTHING TOXIC ABOUT IT "

(MANLY HIGH PITCHED SCREAM ECHOES IN THE DISTANCE)

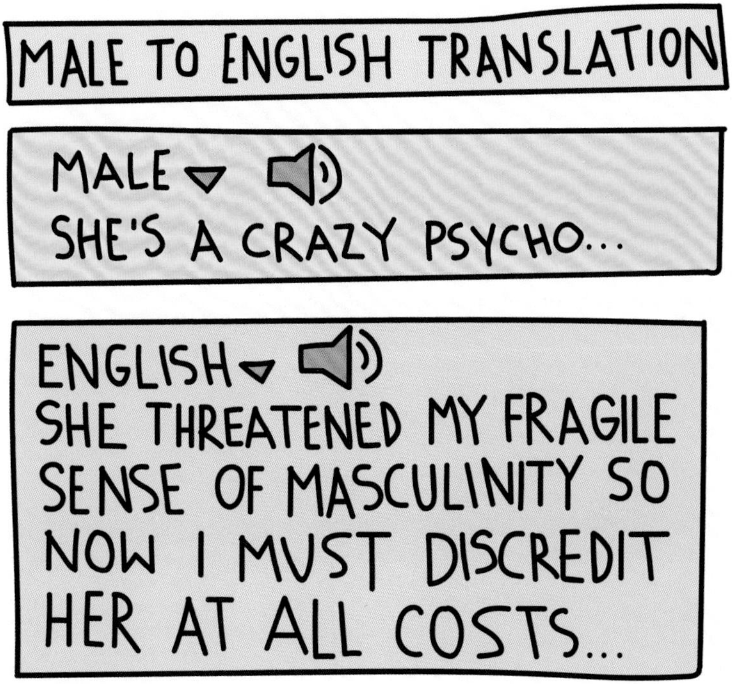

MALE TO ENGLISH TRANSLATION

MALE ▽ 🔊
SHE'S A CRAZY PSYCHO...

ENGLISH ▽ 🔊
SHE THREATENED MY FRAGILE
SENSE OF MASCULINITY SO
NOW I MUST DISCREDIT
HER AT ALL COSTS...

REMINDER:
TODDLERS CAN'T READ

A VERY MASCULINE COLOUR PALETTE

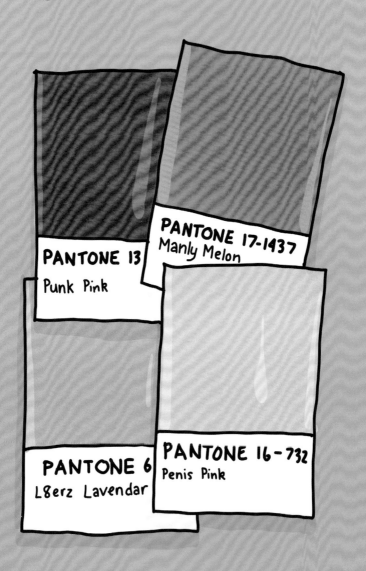

EXPECTATION:
manhood

REALITY:

manh~~ooooood~~

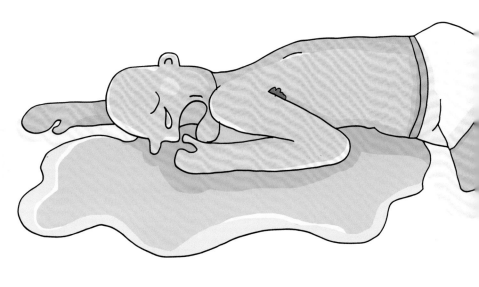

CRY LIKE A MAN

19/10/18

A VERY MANLY TO-DO LIST

- READ A GOOD BOOK
- GO FOR A WALK
- CALL GRANDMA ♥
- LEARN FRENCH (???)
- BAKE A LEMON SPONGE CAKE
- LISTEN TO SAD SONGS AND HAVE A BIG-ASS CRY

- CHECK IN WITH MATES ABOUT NOTHING IN PARTICULAR ☺

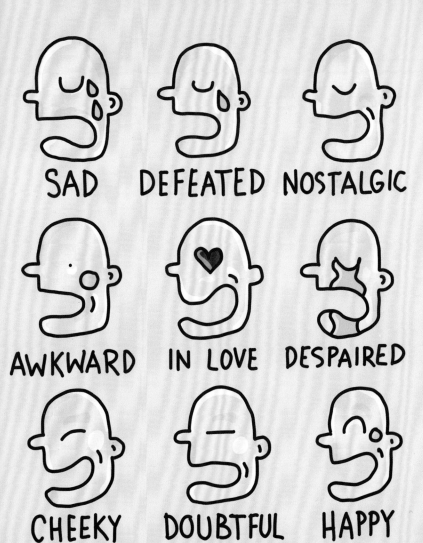

HOW A MAN SHOULD LOOK

REAL HOUSEWIFE OF _____

A BIG STRONG MAN'S GUILTY PLEASURE

A VERY MANLY ALTERCATION

Google
Why are men
why are men so needy
why are men insecure
why are men players

- COUNTRY GENTLEMAN -

Wanted...
More Men Like Mike!

A LOVE OF NATURE!

NOT AFRAID TO CRY!

RESPECTS WOMEN!

GENTLE + KIND!

MINDFUL!

U. S. ARMY

A VERY ACCURATE VENN DIAGRAM

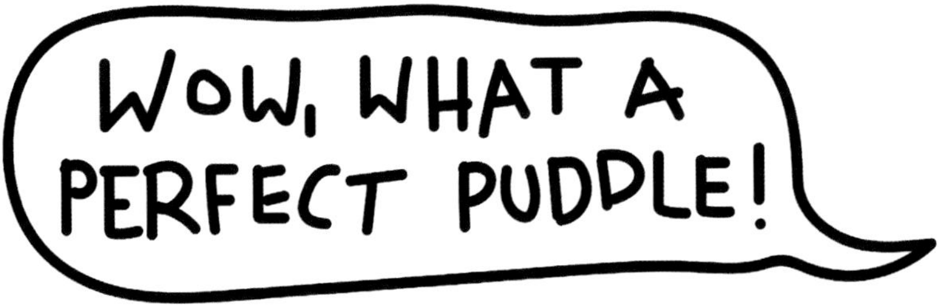
WOW, WHAT A PERFECT PUDDLE!

IMAGINE IF...

A WOMAN
[AN OPINION]

A MAN
[COMPLETE SILENCE]

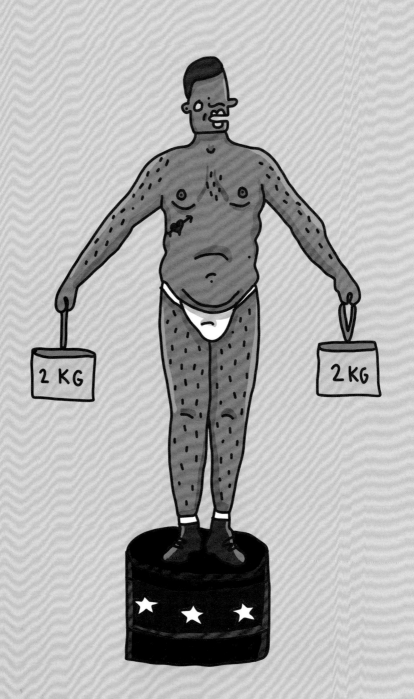

COMMENTATOR 1: I'M GETTING WORD THAT HE HAS SUFFERED A DEBILITATING PANIC ATTACK...

COMMENTATOR 2: POOR FELLA...

A VERY MANLY MAGNET SET

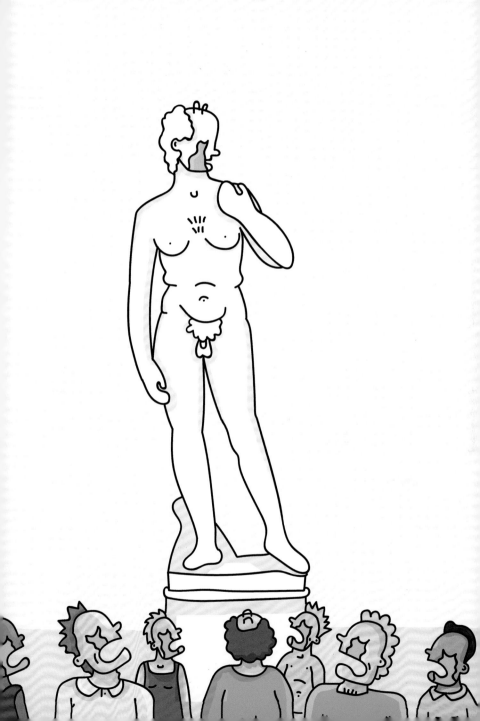

A VERY STRONG-WORDED, MANLY TEXT MESSAGE

HOW MASCULINE IS A MAN WHO...

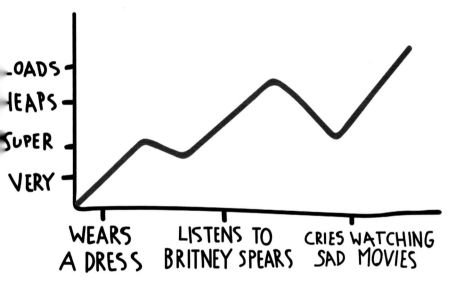

THE PYRAMID OF MASCULINITY

DON'T SWEAT THE SMALL STUFF

AN (ALMOST) VENN DIAGRAM

Published in 2019 by Smith Street Books
Melbourne | Australia
smithstreetbooks.com

ISBN: 978-1-925811-15-5

Publisher: Paul McNally
Project editor: Patrick Boyle
Design & layout: Murray Batten

Printed & bound in China by C&C Offset Printing Co., Ltd.

Book 93
10 9 8 7 6 5 4 3 2 1